Harvest Festival

T0362821

Myanmar Celebrates

This is rice.

My family grows rice.

3

Look at the rice.

My mum plants the rice.

Look at the rice.

The rice grows in water.

Look at the rice.

My dad cuts the rice.

Look at the rice.

The rice will dry in the sun.

11

Look at the rice now.

We make this with the rice.

Yum! Yum!

Rice is special to us.